How to Make a Boring Subject **Interesting**

52 ways even a nerd can be heard

GENI WHITEHOUSE

This title may be purchased for business or promotional use or for special
sales. For information, please e-mail **bulksales@uptonblanding.com**.

Published by Upton and Blanding Associates, Pleasanton, CA,
www.uptonblanding.com

Cover Design and Layout: Adina Cucicov
Editor: Amy Moore, **www.moorewords.com**
Illustrations: Mary Patterson, **www.fishchild.com**

ISBN: 978-0-692-00151-6
First Printing 2009, Printed in the United States of America.

Author's website www.EvenANerd.com

Dedication

In memory of Susan Sheridan Austin,
the best presenter I have ever known.

and

To Chip and Mary Beth who have spent
most of their lives fruitlessly trying
to de-nerdify their Mom but who manage
to support and inspire me anyway.

Table of Contents

INTRODUCTION

No subject is boring to *everyone*.

Likewise, no subject is inherently interesting to everyone. Rather, it's about the relationship between the communicator and the listener.

The secret to communication and presentation success lies in finding a subject that is interesting to you and making it interesting to your audience.

That's what this book is about.

This book is for presenters who want to have more fun with their material, who want to find a way to connect with their audience, who want to be heard.

Often presenters who are saddled with boring subjects get labeled boring by virtue of association. That's what has happened to entire professions like accounting, actuarial science, and funeral management.

But it doesn't have to be the case. This book will help you find and create the interesting in every subject.

The boring versus interesting call is pretty subjective. There is no procedural checklist you can follow every time.

There are lots of elements involved in good communication and when any one of them is missing, you can quickly slip into boring territory.

Sometimes it's a timing thing. *(Ever been to a networking event immediately following your arrival on a red-eye flight? Nothing anyone says is going to keep you awake for long.)*

Other times it's a delivery issue. *(The presenter speaks in a monotone.)* It could be a matter of failing to meet expectations or providing too much information. *(I thought this was a 30 minute show—you mean I have to tune in next week to see the conclusion?)*

Or it could be that your audience is full of beginners and your material is advanced. *(I wanted to learn how to tune an engine, not build one.)*

Your goal, if you are the presenter, is to find out as much as you can about your audience and create a presentation that is perfectly suited to them.

Every subject is interesting to *somebody.* I am sure there is at least one person who is interested in the gestation period of an armadillo. (Actually, according to Google there are about 11,700 people interested enough in this topic to mention it.) But, there is an element of luck in finding a second person who is interested in that same subject.

When you want your message to reach more than three people, it's time to get serious. It's time to read this book.

This book focuses on the message. There are plenty of other great books on presenting that you should read too. (See the appendix.)

But this book, the one written lovingly for you by this nerd, will take you through 11 different areas that influence the power of your message.

It includes 52 ideas to help you find new sources of inspiration and new ways to organize your material. Some of the tips might even get you to take a risk, to be more edgy than you've been in the past. Before you're through, you might even discover that you enjoy making presentations.

You might be wondering why I chose to write this book for nerds.

In High School, I lettered in Algebra II. (You think I'm kidding.)

I am a nerd. When you are a nerd, there are only a couple of career options. So of course I became an accountant. During the course of my career, one of the things I have learned is that people in business rely on us nerds.

In fact, there is a nerdy engine that powers most successful businesses. Business owners need accountants. Salespeople need engineers. Software vendors need software developers. Wineries need wine makers. Drug companies need chemists. Astronauts need NASA engineers to put them in orbit. Occasionally, we might even need to consult with a medical professional who specializes in say, spasmodic dysplasia.

The point is that anyone who is immersed in a unique specialty is what I would consider a "nerd" at least in that subject, and they probably have valuable insights to share with the rest of us.

This book is about helping them find their voice.

WHERE TO BEGIN?

*As Far Away From Your
Computer As Possible*

Most writers will tell you that they hate to face the blank page. And it's no wonder. It's easy to feel paralyzed at the beginning of a project.

The white screen or page is like a mirror for your brain: completely devoid of thoughts. The flashing cursor is a menacing little bug. If it had a voice it would be saying, *"Take a break. Do something else. I hate this. I'd like a donut."*

That's why I like to redefine the beginning. When you're preparing for a presentation, don't expect to open up a blank slide deck and just start typing.

Start somewhere else. Your first steps don't necessarily involve a forced lock-down in your chair running through all of the facts that relate to your presentation.

The best ideas come to me when I'm away from the topic. I spend a little bit of time consciously thinking about the parameters of the problem, and then I leave it alone for a while.

Sometimes I even start in the middle. There might be one really amazing idea, insight, or image that jumps right out from the middle of my subject and then I am able to add content before and after that.

As I am out and about, I'm better able to put myself in the place of the audience. I always get inspiration on airplanes—probably because they're the only place you don't get interrupted by one of those marvels of modern technology.

So give yourself time to ponder. Start by focusing on the idea, the emotion, or the reason you are making a presentation. Then follow these tips before you try to create your slides, script or handouts.

Create a one-pager.

*And I'm not talking about one of those nerdy
devices you have clipped to your belt.*

If you can describe all of the pertinent information about your subject on one piece of paper, then you can turn it into a presentation. Just start writing. Don't try to edit yourself at the beginning.

Your goal is to create what Betsy Burroughs likes to call "a lousy first draft."[1] Then you can start playing with your content to create a one-page document.

If you haven't tried to do this, particularly on your favorite subject, you'll be surprised to learn how difficult it is to condense everything that you want to say onto one page.

But the exercise of dumping all of your information on paper and then editing it down to a single page is extremely valuable. It will really help you choose the correct words and will give you great clarity around what information is most vital to your message.

Once you have the one-pager, you have the option of adding details to form an informative handout, or paring it down further to form the basis of your presentation. Which conveniently leads me to my next point.

---

1 Betsy Burroughs, www.focuscatalyst.com, author of *FOCUS. The Catalyst for Creativity. In your work. In your life.*

Identify your top three message points.

Why three? Ask Goldilocks' bears, those little pigs, or the blind mice.

Identify your top three message points.

Not to compare your audience to fidgety preschoolers at storytelling hour, but the number three works for fairy tales and public speeches for the simple reason that two is too few and four too many.

And three means there is a beginning, a middle, and an end. We accountants like balance and symmetry and three works perfectly. (Although I really like 2, and 4 is an even number, and 42 is a significant number, and 17 is prime.)

It's important to identify your top three message points. These three little gems will be your agenda for the presentation. You don't have to specifically list them but your audience should be able to repeat them at the conclusion of your session.

Before you define your top three message points, you'll need to ask yourself some questions and make sure you have well-articulated answers.

If you don't, you may find yourself creating an aimless or confusing presentation. In other words, a boring presentation.

So ask—and answer—yourself:

- Why am I speaking?
- What do I know about the audience?
- What am I trying to accomplish?
- What do I want people to walk away knowing?
- What should they do after they hear my words of wisdom?
- Why does my audience care about this?

Answering these questions will help you create a clear picture of your end goal and your audience's expectations. Now that you know where you're going, you're ready to figure out how to get there.

Make a list of all your message points and test them against your end-goal. Keep pruning until you have three.

3

Use a mind mapping™ technique to generate ideas for your topic.

Because you don't want those great ideas getting lost in your mind.

Mind mapping is one of those tricks the creative types have been keeping from the rest of us for years.

It is a great way to loosen up your brain and generate ideas. I learned the secret from Jeff Justice, my stand-up comedy instructor in Atlanta, Georgia.

Here's how it works.

First, think of a single word or simple picture that encapsulates your topic.

Then:

- Put your word or picture in the middle of a blank sheet of paper and draw a circle around it.

- Draw at least three branches extending out from the circle.

- At the end of each branch, write down the first word or picture that comes to mind.

- Keep drawing branches off of branches, and keep your hand moving.

- The very act of drawing a branch will force your mind to supply a word at the end of it. So draw a branch even if you don't know what you're going to write next.

(If you want to learn more about this technique there are a number of books on the subject including *The Mind Map Book: How to Use Radiant Thinking to Maximize Your Brain's Untapped Potential*, by Tony Buzan.)

Note the use of the magic number three. (See Tip 2.) The mind works in threes, so make sure you always draw three branches and stretch yourself to fill them in.

If you have Microsoft® Visio® software, you can create a mind map on your computer. Look for the mind mapping templates under flowcharting.

If you get stuck, try searching Google or www.flickr.com for inspiration.

At the end of this exercise, you should end up with some interesting ideas about where to take your presentation.

Here is a Visio mind map I created for a presentation on auditing. This exercise led me to the idea of creating a business presentation called, *"How to keep your company from being the next exhibit at the fraud museum."*

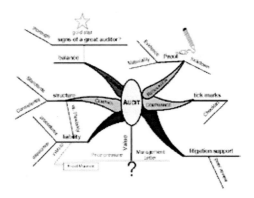

A MATTER OF ENTITLEMENT

Finding the Right Title for Your Presentation

When I was working on the journalism staff at my high school newspaper, I labored for hours over the headline.

A good headline had to be both compelling—so it could grab the reader's attention—and concise, so it could fit in whatever space was allocated.

Just like headlines for newspaper articles, presentation titles are important because they "sell" your message. If the title doesn't grab your readers or your audience, they aren't going to stick around to hear whatever you are trying to say.

I think coming up with a good title is the fun part of crafting a presentation. You get to switch to the un-nerdy side of your brain and dig for some creative insights.

Sometimes the title comes first and then the presentation follows. Other times, you get all of your ideas for a message fully formed and then the snappy title comes to mind.

A good title can keep people guessing and can even be the memorable scrap of information that allows other people to spread your message for you. So keep it short but make it memorable.

The tips that follow are some of the approaches I've used to come up with my own little piece of entitlement.

Count on numbers.

Numbers aren't always boring. Where do most
people love to see numbers?
In song titles: 50 Ways to Leave Your Lover
In late-night TV: Letterman's top 10
On book covers: Like this one

You get the idea. Titles that incorporate a number are one of the most popular ways to get a reader's attention.

Try using this approach for your topic. Use a Top 10 list or similar framework to organize your message—but make sure you keep your audience's perspective in mind.

Actually, I try to stay away from the number 10. I like to use other numbers because 10 has been so over done. Try 7 or 11 or even 17.5*. Any number can be used as the basis for a good presentation.

By the way, this method works especially well for accountants. Their world is numbers. So if they are your audience—it's gonna be a slam dunk.

(Note my clever use of sports analogies. Sports analogies always work for male audiences or UNC Tarheels. This is actually a free tip included at no extra charge.)

---

* This number comes from Mark Severance, Director of Sales & Marketing at Arxis Technology. He had me deliver this topic at an event: *"17.5 Ways Even a Nerd Can be Heard"*. It was pretty hard to find ".5" of something to talk about. At least he didn't make me go to three decimal places.

Recycle, reuse, repurpose.

"Nerds of a feather flock together."

Are there some expressions you've heard one too many times? Try repurposing them to serve your own selfish needs.

Why start from scratch when you can take someone else's tired over-used topic and convert it to a title for your next presentation?

I live in Northern California, so if I hear about global warming or "going green" one more time I might just scream.

But in an effort to save my sanity, I might just do a presentation called *"Stop Global Boring"* about teaching scientists to make better presentations.

Same topic, but delivered to a room full of accountants? Since my fellow accountants are constantly talking about GAAP or Generally Accepted Accounting Principles*, I might title my presentation *"Generally Accepted Presentation Principles."* Who says you have to be totally original?

Sick of hearing *"think outside of the box"?* How about *"think outside of the Milky Way"* for your next presentation at a Star Wars convention?

I've got a million of these things** on my blog…

* Reason #1265 you might want to avoid accountants at a dinner party.
** Reason #472 you might want to avoid me at a dinner party.

Use juxtapositioning to your advantage.

If you find yourself in a Scrabble game and want to use "juxtapose" it is worth a whopping 25 points. You can send me my 5-point commission (or just the letter K) if you use it.

Juxtapositioning means putting two unrelated ideas together. And as useful as it is for Scrabble, it's an even more useful idea for creating a compelling presentation title.

By placing two items that you would never expect (or frankly hope) to see in the same sentence together, you make your audience curious. They'll be dying to know, *"How in the world is he/she going to tie these two items together?"*

One of my favorite examples of juxtapositioning is the "Shoes and Cheese Store" that actually exists in Tennessee. What were the owners of that store thinking? The only common bond I can come up with is smell—both cheese and shoes have a distinctive odor.

I still regret never actually going in that store to find out how they merged these two items. I can only hope that the cheese was not tucked into various shoes so that you could sample your favorite Asiago while you were trying on a nice pair of Bandolinos. And talk about pairings. *"Does Swiss or Gouda go better with these Hushpuppy loafers?"*

You can see how the art of juxtapositioning can open up worlds of possibilities and get the creative juices flowing for a great presentation.

Let your audience be the judge.

"Brown vs. The Board of Education"
"Roe v. Wade"

If it works for the Supreme Court,
it can work for you.

Let's say you are trying to make a point on a particular subject. Give your presentation a title that befits a court case and you'll intrigue your audience from the beginning. They'll expect you to show both sides of the argument in your presentation (and of course you'll deliver.)

List all of the pros and all of the cons and then let your audience reach their own conclusions. You might even treat them like the jury at a trial.

Of course, you need to find plenty of information that supports your point of view. And it wouldn't hurt if the opposing arguments were on the weak side. Hey, this isn't a matter of life or death. We're talking about a presentation here.

By the way, this is a great example of how your choice of title can drive the whole format of your presentation—making it interesting from beginning to end.

TRIMMING THE FAT

*Sometimes It Takes a Sharp Knife
and a Critical Eye*

t's not just about adding humor and stories to your presentation to make it more interesting. You also need to subtract the boring stuff.

Obviously, some of the boring stuff is your content and you can't have the whole presentation be jokes and anecdotes.

But some of that boring information needs to be taken out or at least diluted by the addition of some other more interesting and relevant content.

As the expert on your topic, you're going to have to take a long hard look at yourself and separate what's meaningful to you from what's meaningful to your audience.

If you're me or one of my accounting brethren, that means you have to decide if you really need to share that wonderful story about searching for the missing penny while reconciling your bank statement.

If the penny was the key to unraveling a riveting case of embezzlement, then by all means, include the story in your talk about fraud.

But if the penny turned out to be a missing cent when you adjusted your bank balance, you might want to keep that story to yourself or wait to share it with a kindred spirit at your next numismatology* conference.

You even need to subtract the fun information or jokes that don't contribute to or relate to your topic in any way.

While not boring per se, these tidbits are extraneous, and can take away from your message and drain your audience. Have you ever heard someone begin their presentation with an old, tired joke that had nothing to do with the topic? Talk about a waste of time.

* The practice of collecting coins and an example of what not to do. See my Tip #10, below.

Never start your presentation with, *"First, here's some housekeeping."*

I don't do housekeeping at home, what makes you think I want to do it at your event?

Maybe you have some boring stuff you need to tell your conference attendees about the restrooms, the lunch break, and changes to the agenda for the day. Take a cue from the airlines or the movie theaters and find a way to convey your information in a visual or entertaining way.

Does anyone actually listen to the flight attendants giving instructions any more?

They do when they're flying on Southwest because every once in a while you'll get a comedian attendant who will throw in some funny comments and keep everyone listening.

It doesn't have to be funny. Just make it different. Try using a voice from the back as if God is talking to the crowd.

Never use words when a picture will do.

A picture is worth a thousand numbers.

Which has more impact?

"It was cold."

Or

10

Avoid jargon.

*"Jargon" would make a great name for a pet.
"Watch out for Jargon. He bites and has
a nasty temper."*

Let's say you have to share financial information with non-financial people. Don't use accounting jargon.

One man's meaningful jargon is another man's reason to zone out into space.

Weird, unidentified words jumping off of your slide can cause your audience to totally obsess about that one word they don't understand until they create their own brain cramp and decide to stop listening to you. But enough about me.

If you're an accountant, you probably don't want to use references to the General Ledger, GAAP (Generally Accepted Accounting Principles), or amortization in your presentation. These are terms that normal people just don't use in regular conversation so keep them out of your presentation.

I attended a wine industry conference and listened to a wine expert talk about brix, micro-oxygenation, and lactic acid. These subjects were perfectly acceptable when presented to a group of other wine experts, but wouldn't be appropriate if the presenter were trying to sell wine to a group of visiting tourists.

Instead, use plain English to translate jargon into terms your audience can understand. You may have to use a sentence instead of a single word.

Here's an example:

Accountant to husband: *"How much did you contribute to your 401(k) plan this year? And did you update your W-4?"*

Husband to accountant: *"I don't know but my company kept $200 per month for my retirement savings, and I had to fill out another one of those forms to tell my company to take out more taxes."*

AAIAAP

Avoid Acronyms If At All Possible.

Those acronyms that are a normal part of your daily conversation don't mean anything to your audience unless they happen to be IM* addicts like my children—in which case, you're doomed anyway.

As an employee of a software company, I was once quoted talking about VARs for an article in an accounting trade publication. I got a nasty note from a CPA (Certified Public Accountant), telling me that he didn't know what a VAR was, and I should explain my terms. A VAR is a "Value Added Reseller" and I shall never again fail to explain what I am talking about.

Acronyms are essentially jargon, and you should use them with the same caution advised in Tip #10. Using acronyms on slides can cause certain members of your audience to spend all of their time and energy guessing what the letters represent.

As long as those letters are on the screen, they won't hear all of your wonderful points. Eventually, IMHO**, they will just take out their pocket Sudoku game and resort to numbers in an attempt to restore order to their universe.

* Instant Messaging
** In My Humble Opinion

Put the boring stuff on handouts.

"Slip-slidin' away..."
—Paul Simon, singing about your audience
if you don't follow this tip.

If there is some information that is detailed (read "boring"), but nonetheless important to your audience, write it down and hand it out at the end of your presentation.

That's why some smart nerd invented spreadsheets: they lend themselves beautifully to handy tables comparing all forms of products, solutions, and ideas. So put it on a spreadsheet and keep it off your slides.

Got a whole bunch of website addresses you want to share with your audience? Write them down or put them on your website and send your audience to that page.

Have you ever listened to someone reading out a bunch of website addresses? It sounds like this: "W-W-W-DOT-I-am-a-boring-speaker-DOT-COM."

Know where to draw the line.

"I walk the line."
—Johnny Cash, singing
about how to stay true to yourself—
but truer to your audience.

At some point you have to be able to a draw a line between the information that is meaningful and all of that other stuff you just happen to know about a particular subject.

If your goal is to make your presentation interesting, then you have to filter the information that you share.

If your goal is to prove that you are the international expert on the mating habits of the mourning dove, then by all means, share everything you know. Just ignore any snoring that you might hear during your presentation.

Here's where to draw the line:

Interesting and meaningful to everyone

Interesting to me—boring to everyone else

PLUGGING IN

The Joy of Seeing the Lights Come On

A message that isn't heard isn't really a successful message, is it?

But the members of your audience are a little hard of hearing—deafened by the sound of their inner thoughts and the noise of a million competing messages.

So unless your message can break through that noise and distraction and find its way to your listener, you might as well be talking to yourself. And then all of your hours of preparation and learning will have been for naught. Now I'm just depressing myself.

How do you break through? By connecting with your audience.

This is the cardinal rule of being interesting. Establishing a relationship with your audience is the number one priority for every interaction—whether it's a one-on-one conversation with your children, a bridge game with three of your friends, or a speech delivered from the podium to a gathering of thousands.

All of the great speakers in history mastered the art of connecting with their audience.

In the tips that follow, I'll show you how to build the kinds of connections that will help you enlighten your audience—and maybe even yourself.

Make it personal.

Know thyself. You don't have to be an employee of ORACLE to know this is important.

In order to make any subject interesting, you have to be able to draw from your own experiences, tell a good story, and deliver it with energy.

Start with what you have. Make your unique qualities your competitive advantage. Embrace all of your quirks and harness them as key presentation tools.

Watch Ellen Degeneres. She is at her funniest when she stutters, stammers, and blunders her way to a point. And her topics can be about totally mundane events or occurrences.

Your goal is to identify some perspective from your own life that allows you to empathize with your audience.

That's easy to do if you are presenting to a group of controllers, and you have been in that job. But what if you are a controller presenting to CEOs?

As a former controller, what experience could you draw on to help you relate to the CEO's perspective? Well, have you ever run a business or division, coached a softball team, or organized an event? Then there are comparisons that you can draw.

Have you ever tried to herd cattle? Watched a flock of geese? Seen a group of baby birds following their mother? Then you might know what a CEO feels like at various times during the day.

The point is that first you have to think about who you are, where you have been, and what you know. Then you need to think about who your listeners are, what matters to them, and what they know.

And then you have to look for the point of intersection. Don't worry if the connection doesn't come right away. Stretch your mind. Reach for it. It will come.

Put yourself in their shoes.

And hopefully, they don't wear a size five.
Because then all you're gonna be
thinking about is pain.

Put yourself in their shoes.

Start with your subject and then begin to think of all the ways it might impact the members of your audience.

What is it about that subject that is going to make an impact on their daily lives?

Will it change how they approach that stack of paperwork piled up on their desk?

Will it subject them to scrutiny that wasn't there before?

Will it make their company more important in the eyes of their customers?

Does it affect their ability to hire?

Will it make their goods and services more expensive to deliver?

Cheaper to deliver?

Relating your topic to your audience is the absolute key to making a memorable presentation. If you don't get this right, nothing else matters.

If your subject matter is boring, but critical—i.e. not knowing about it can send your audience members to prison—it will probably be a little more interesting to them.

But don't assume. You need to know their perspective before you start talking.

If your audience consists of controllers and the topic you are presenting, say Sarbanes-Oxley, mandates that they lose their bonus in the event they sign off on an erroneous financial statement, you might have an angle.

Do you think these people are going to sleep during your presentation? I don't care if you have 100 slides with just black text on a white background, as the expert on this subject in a room full of controllers, you're going to be riveting.

Now if you're presenting to a room full of sales people on this same subject, you're going to have to try a different approach. You are going to have to find a way to connect this subject to their next commission check. Do you think the top salespeople at Enron got their last commission check?

Am I asking you to think on your feet? Not if those shoes are too tight. You should always be able to make an educated guess about who your audience is ahead of "show time." If not, be flexible—and yes, think on your feet.

Know what is top of mind for your audience right now.

"Price of pigs feet drops $5. Local pig farmers turning to other body parts for revenue."
—The Hogville Daily Tribune

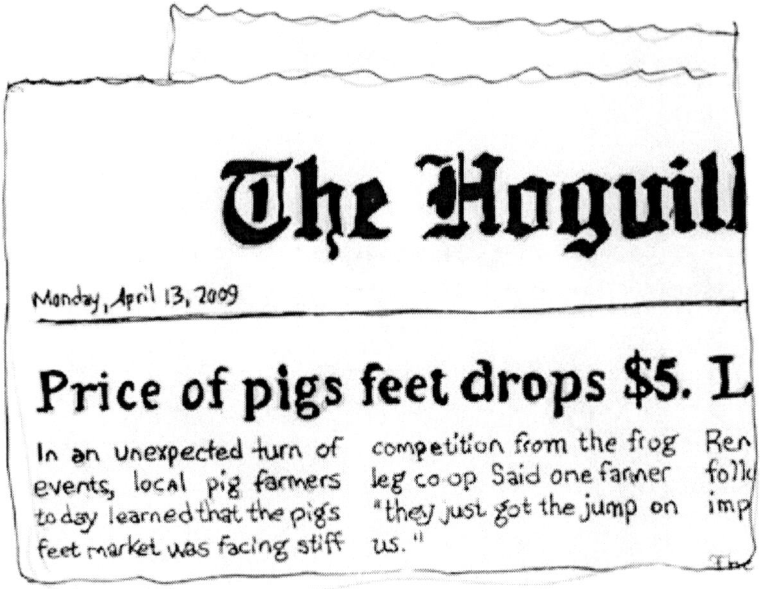

The Hoguill

Monday, April 13, 2009

Price of pigs feet drops $5. L

In an unexpected turn of events, local pig farmers today learned that the pigs feet market was facing stiff competition from the frog leg co-op Said one farmer "they just got the jump on us."

Ren
foll
imp

If this is the headline in the local paper and you are the keynote presenter on a topic called "Planning for Retirement," you might want to find a way to talk about pig's feet. (What I wouldn't give to find myself in just such a predicament with this kind of material.)

Can you imagine your opening slide? How about a piggy bank without its feet?

The point is, you need to know what is going on with members of your audience right now. Today. What are they wrestling with in their daily jobs? What are their frustrations?

Your message needs to be tailored so that it resonates with them—wherever they happen to be standing in that moment.

In the case of those farmers in Hogville, you probably don't want to know what they've been standing in.

17

Imagine everyone in the room is trying to blackmail you.

I frequently imagine that everyone in the audience knows my sister, Lynn, who will tell them about that time I got a fork stuck in my lip in elementary school.

Blackmail?

Yes. Think about it. What if everyone in the audience had access to one dirty little secret about your product, your idea, your concept, or your company?

How do you take the sting out of being blackmailed? You disclose the secret and take away the blackmailer's power. So do the same thing for your presentation.

Figure out all of the potential negatives that you don't want your audience to discover and share them. Get them out of the way so you can focus on the other more positive messages.

Otherwise, that one person in the room who has some killer question about your known problem is going to jump up and make you lose credibility.

I don't want to sound paranoid here, but I have seen people trying to ignore that potential stink bomb and then when it goes off they pay a big price.

If you don't have any potential issues, defensive attendees, or well-known counter-arguments to your position that could be used to reduce the power of your message, then go have a glass of champagne to celebrate your good fortune.

If you have surveyed your potential partners and they keep telling you that your inventory solution is missing a key feature, you can't try to hide that.

Tell your audience that you know about the missing feature and describe your plan to address it. Then you can launch into all of the other great features that you have without shame or fear of questions.

After all, connecting with your audience means thinking about their concerns—and showing that you've done so by addressing them in a forthright way.

Adapt your presentation to fit the style of the listener.

"Welcome to short-attention-span theater."
—Marquee on CEO's forehead

You're a nerd. You like details.

He's the CEO. He likes short and sweet.

It's probably a good idea for one of you to compromise. It probably won't be the CEO.

You walk into the CEO's office. His desk is clear with not a single piece of paper on it. He asks you to give him your recommendations on an acquisition target.

After spending days researching, analyzing, charting, graphing, pivot-tabling, and auto-filtering your way through 14 Excel spreadsheets, you now feel comfortable—well as comfortable as you will ever be, given the fact that today is the deadline— recommending that the acquisition of this company go through.

Your natural inclination is to bring to the meeting every single piece of paper representing every piece of research that supports your position. After all, he might ask you a question that you can't answer.

Fight that impulse with every ounce of your being.

Be short and concise and only provide the facts. You can always provide more details if asked for them. The CEO doesn't want to hear any details. He wants to rely on your judgment.

Never make the assumption that your audience members are interested in how you arrived at your conclusion. They only need to understand that your conclusion is based on fact and they need to feel confident that you can support your idea if the need arises.

Work with the differences.

*"What is a sales pipeline?" said
the accountant at a presentation about
sales and accounting software.*

*"What is a pro-forma P & L?" said the sales
person, at the same presentation.*

Understand the differences between you and your listeners. Make fun of the differences to get a good laugh and to show you "get it." Then put your money where your mouth is by adapting your communication style to theirs.

Take an accountant presenting to salespeople, for example. (Gee, where did Geni get that example?)

These are two groups that are often on different ends of the same spectrum.

Accountants are the people charged with reviewing a salesperson's expense report, collecting on their sales, and holding them accountable for a bunch of paperwork.

And while accountants understand the importance of having someone drive the revenues for a business, they are often astounded by the amount of commission they pay their sales force.

Make fun of these qualities, and you'll win over a sales crowd in two seconds.

But not so fast, Mr. Salesman. Your people, on the other hand, view accountants as the only obstacle preventing their next big sale. There is always another form to fill out, another credit report to be completed, and another exception to producing that commission check you are due.

Okay, you understand both perspectives. Now what?

Let's start with the accountant presenting to salespeople. Having read Tip #18, I know that I need to adapt my presentation to the preferences of my listener. So I'm going to look for a non-accounting way to present information to this audience. Hey, how about charts and maps? Sales people love those!

Now, if I am the salesperson presenting to accountants, I'm going to do the opposite and play off of their perceptions of salespeople as golf playing beer-guzzling buffoons who don't work very hard. (No offense to any salespeople out there.) And I'll make sure I've got the data to back up my points.

How to Please a Salesperson:
A Nifty Nerd Tool

Say you want to show George in sales that he really didn't sell a single unit in North Dakota this month. Create your spreadsheet showing sales results by salesperson, territory, etc., and then import that spreadsheet into Microsoft MapPoint.

You can reconcile all of the numbers to your heart's content in the spreadsheet, and still present a visual tool that George can understand.

Work with the similarities.

Great minds think alike.

If you're the preacher, and are preaching to the choir, then sprinkle your presentation with insider comments. Talk about other members of the parish, or mention quirks of your building, area, or neighborhood. Describe commonly known or shared tools that relate to your topic.

Rather than overwhelming your audience with your impressive bio, craft stories that describe your own experiences while allowing you to share your credentials. Mention past roles that would resonate with your audience.

So if you are an accountant talking to accountants, talk about debits and credits. Talk about how hard it is to work with salespeople, how much you love Excel, or how crazy it gets at the end of the month.

Or use backgrounds that are cut from green ledger paper, hand out green eyeshades and ask them to spot the out-of-balance item on the slide.

They love the same stuff you love. We all wear our black socks to the beach. We all had to count cash and send out audit confirmations.

And haven't we all debated the benefits of .5 Pentel lead for our mechanical pencils over the .7 variety? Or is that just me? Does anyone still use pencils?

If you're interested, .5 Pentel is best.

21

Research local customs.

"If you talk to a man in a language he understands, that goes to his head. If you talk to him in his language, that goes to his heart."
—*Nelson Mandela*

You suddenly find yourself scheduled to speak to a crowd of business people about accounting software in South Africa.

Thankfully, the software is the same product that you know in the US, but you don't know much about accounting differences or the local customs.

Look for a way to establish a connection and then weave threads throughout your material.

From the South to South Africa . . .

Yes, this example is from my experience and here's how researching local customs helped me connect with an audience in a very unfamiliar culture. In my case, said "research" was conducted via my stomach.

Being a product of the southern U.S., I find that food is not only a central part of my life, but it is also a key tool for breaking down cultural barriers.

Imagine my surprise, while dining in South Africa, to be served what looked to me to be grits. I later found out that this corn-ground delicacy was in fact the same thing as grits, but was called "pup" in South Africa.

The locals displayed a frightening tendency to put gravy and sauces on their grits, but I chose to ignore that infraction. I had discovered a culinary bond to my friends in South Africa.

Next, I was taken to a special roadside stand where we purchased what looked to me to be beef jerky.

Now if you haven't been seen driving on a dirt road gnawin' on a chunk of beef jerky, you're probably not from the South.

In South Africa, this delicacy is called "biltong" and is occasionally made from "kudu" rather than beef. But again, using literary license, it was close enough for me to build a connection.

So with my two new-found connections, I constructed a presentation called "Communicating Financial Information" which began with images of these items and others.

I asked the audience to name the images. Each time they gave me their local term and I instructed them on the proper Southern or US terminology.

My point was to establish a common understanding, which was essentially a demo for the theme for the rest of my presentation.

I then went on to illustrate how my software could be used to provide a similar level of shared understanding for non-financial consumers of financial statements.

22

Sell it before you tell it.

"The fact is, everyone is in sales.
Whatever area you work in, you do have clients
and you do need to sell."
—Jay Abraham

A big part of delivering a successful presentation comes from exceeding your audience's expectations.

That means you have to first set their expectations. And that is where the introductory blurb comes in.

Often, the hardest part of giving a presentation is deciding what to say in that all-important introductory sales paragraph. Typically you have to commit to that paragraph well in advance of your presentation.

Many times, you write it with full insight into what you plan to say, and then you change your mind before you make your presentation.

As long as you deliver at least as much as you promised, you will not disappoint your audience, but there are some traps you need to consider:

What will your attendees learn? Make sure you tell them what new skills they will acquire. What insights will they gain?

What level of information are you providing? if you promise "advanced material" and deliver "basic" your audience will be disappointed. Likewise if you position your session as basic and then deliver advanced material you won't have many fans.

Who is your session designed for? People who have never used a computer? Or people who have designed their own website?

My blurbs follow a pattern. They start with a general statement, usually tied to something going on in current events. Then I tell the attendees what they will learn, and what they will take away from my session.

Here's a sample :

Doing More With Less: 7 Ways to Recession-Proof Your Business

We can't change the economy but we can help you change your odds of surviving in it. In this session, we'll show you how the principles of Kaizen and the art of doing more with less can make any operation more efficient. We'll help you decide where to focus, what information your bankers want to see, and where to cut costs. You'll learn how empowering your team can lead to permanent improvements and you'll leave this session with 7 ideas you can apply to the challenges you face in your own business.

MARY POPPINS WAS RIGHT

*You Need at Least a Spoonful of Sugar
to Make the Boring Stuff Go Down*

Have you ever seen those cookbooks for kids that say to puree spinach and bake it into brownies? (We're not talking about THOSE brownies.) As if that's the only way you can get your kids to eat their vegetables!

Well, it is. And the same is true for boring subjects. You have to add some sweetener and mix well with the boring stuff.

Get people laughing and the benefits are many:

- Time goes faster
- They'll yawn less because they'll be using their mouth for other things
- They'll give you more 10s on your evaluation
- Lots of people will want to sit with you at lunch
- They will be absolutely stunned to learn that you can make something as boring as (insert your subject) funny.

But most importantly, laughter helps people relax so they can be more receptive to new ideas and information. Here are a few ways I've found to add humor to my presentations.

Look for an oddity or humorous angle.

Eventually, even Melba Toast can be softened with water.

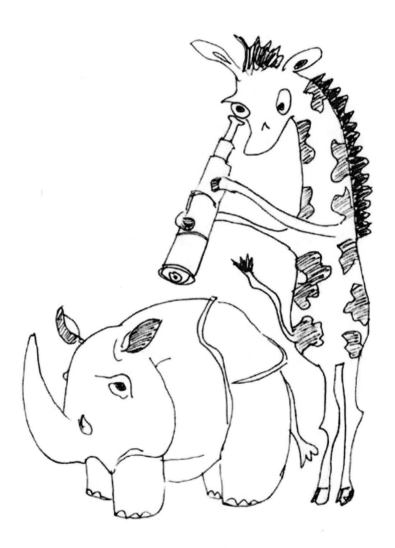

Look for an oddity or humorous angle.

No matter how boring the subject, there is almost always something involved that you can make fun of.

Maybe your subject has a weird name or involves strange rules, or it is imposed using some sort of arcane calculation. Read through your data with an eye for spotting that oddity and use it in your presentation.

I faced this situation when giving a presentation on sales tax. How was I going to make a bunch of tax information interesting? What was I thinking when I agreed to do this presentation?

Well, never fear, the tax code was here with lots of helpful information.

I started searching state tax information and found my way to the Utah exemption listing. It provided about 17 pages of information about how various items were taxed.

When I got to the donut line I knew I had found pay dirt (or at least pay sugar).

It seems that donuts with utensils are taxed differently than donuts that are not in close proximity to said utensils. That just lead me to start wondering exactly what kinds of utensils you needed to eat a donut and it went on from there.

I kept digging and eventually discovered some more interesting tidbits. Did you know that some states tax Dark Chocolate Milky Way bars differently from their Milk Chocolate counterparts? Did you know that size matters when you are determining how to tax a marshmallow?

Well those oddities became the framework for my presentation.

I used photos of named objects as dividers between my key messages and asked the audience to try to determine the difference between items that were taxed differently.

I did this at intervals throughout my message and I didn't hear a single snore during the session.

Try a novel format.

And I don't mean "War and Peace."

Let's say you are assigned the task of educating your customers on how best to work with your technical support department.

You basically have a list of rules and procedures to cover in your 50-minute session. Your content reads like the 10 commandments minus those exciting sins of passion. In other words, it's dry.

You have two choices:

1. You can read through the list, one PowerPoint slide at a time

   Or

2. You can turn your list into "Technical Support Jeopardy" and have your audience guess the right answers for cash and prizes.

25

Tie your message to a season, holiday or local event.

"Rudolph with your nose so bright,
won't you guide my sleigh tonight?"
—Frustrated American Airlines passenger,
seeking alternative means of transportation.

I was making a presentation in a small town to a diverse group of small business owners. I didn't know anything about their roles or their interests, and needed to assume that they didn't know very much about technology.

(Okay, pretend you didn't just hear me say that I made a presentation without knowing much about my audience. Big mistake! Clearly I made this presentation before I learned about my own brilliant tips included in Chapter 4.)

Luckily, it was close to Halloween, so I was able to deliver a session about Web technology built around Halloween objects and websites. I used a Halloween candy theme and talked about the treats available for meeting their electronic commerce needs.

One of my central messages was about building a Web store, so I pointed to an online store that sold a complete selection of redneck false teeth.

Selecting a funny product to sell from my Web store helped me take a dry subject and make it interesting. From there I moved on to a pet costume website,* which also kept the audience entertained.

* www.anniescostumes/pet.htm

Play off any stereotypes for people like you.

Last Sunday, I went to the beach wearing my favorite shorts and black socks and got sand in my pocket protector.

Partly due to the mistakes of fashion described above, accountants are often presumed to be boring.

I had to deliver a presentation to get software resellers excited about working with accountants. So I asked them to close their eyes and picture their ideal travelling companion. Then I asked how many people had pictured their CPA. Of course no hands went up.

Then I asked them to picture who they'd want standing next to them when they opened a letter from the Internal Revenue Service. Guess who they pictured then?

So I talked about the fact that we accountants were not anyone's first choice for an entertaining party, but we were still the number one choice for help on issues related to business and personal finances.

And then I went on to describe the importance of accountants to business owners making decisions and their value as influencers on software purchases.

By acknowledging the stereotype, I was able to reduce its power to keep partners from forming alliances with accountants.

If there is a stereotypical idea about your profession, your product, or your service, harness it and make it part of your presentation. People will relate to the stereotype even as you begin to prove that it doesn't really apply.

Use sarcasm.

*"Of course, I enjoy hearing accountant jokes.
Please tell me one."*

If you want to teach people how to do something, show them what not to do.

For example, if you want to teach sales people to change the way they document their meal and entertainment expenses, you might deliver a presentation called, *"How to get permanently stuck with the tab."*

You want people to be curious enough to attend your session. And you also want to set the expectation before they arrive in the room that this is not going to be your ordinary, run-of-the-mill meeting on expense reports.

So a nice dash of sarcasm should just do the trick. Just make sure it's not mean or demeaning sarcasm.

Don Rickles might be funny but he's a professional and unless you're on his level, keep the sarcasm directed at your topic, not at people.

28

Design your presentation like a can of mixed nuts.

"Now with less than 50% peanuts"
— the Planters peanut guy.

When you buy a can of mixed nuts you don't expect every nut to be a cashew. You know you're going to have some of those filler peanuts. But you know every handful is going to have a good flavor.

The same is true of a good presentation. You can't make every point in a memorable drum roll kind of way—so just be generous in scattering the high points through your presentation.

If you have two funny concepts, slides or images, move the best one to the front, and the second one to the end of your presentation. If you have three funny, really interesting, or cool things to say then make sure they are evenly disbursed. In my sales tax presentation, for example, I start out by comparing taxes on two different sizes of marshmallows and end up talking about donuts. I don't care who you are, food is funny.

Aim for variety and spread the impactful stuff around. Your audience will still leave with an overall positive impression and hopefully just the right amount of salt.

AND THE PLOT THICKENS

Everyone Loves a Good Story

Even before they had decent pencils, people like Aesop figured out how much easier it was to make their point with a good story.

Just think about how much more fun it is to hear an exciting tale about a race between a tortoise and a hare rather than sitting through a lecture about the virtues of being slow and steady.

What are the elements of a good story?

Vivid details. A plot with a beginning, middle and end. Good characters. Location. Descriptions. Themes, life lessons. The elements of suspense and surprise. You can use these same techniques to find and tell stories that can support your message.

Become a narrator.

"It was a dark and stormy night…"

Yesterday as I was struggling to get my reluctant basset hound, Abby, to walk the last few blocks toward home, I realized something. If I take her off of the leash, she will willingly follow me home with her tail wagging and a feeling of empowerment.

If I keep her attached to the leash, I can drag her home by sheer force with frequent stops and possibly interruptions from worried neighbors inquiring as to my reason for dragging this poor animal by the throat.

That's when it hit me. Presentations are exactly the same way. Make people feel like they want to follow you—not that they're being dragged along for their own good—and everyone will have more fun.

What just happened here? I told you a story about my dog. And I snuck in a little lesson about presentations. Stories are incredibly effective mediums for your message.

If you want to find and tell a good story, start by examining your life, your career, your interactions with others and find a link to your topic and your audience. That overlap is prime story territory.

Now that you've found your story, narrate it in first person using as much detail as possible.

Bring it to life in the minds of your listeners. That way your audience will each create their own mental images that will make your presentation vivid. Yes, even more vivid than the best animated clip art.

30

Look for emotions associated with your topic.

"Come on baby, light my fire"
—the Doors.

Generating an emotional response in your audience is one of the best ways to make a lasting impression.

Does "Investing in Your Company's 401(K)" plan make people feel safe and secure? If so there's an emotion to play with.

Find images that evoke that feeling and flash them on the screen in support of your argument to invest in those plans now.

Have you seen those life insurance advertisements that show pictures of children and say something like *"Who will take care of them if something happens to you?"* Once you stop sobbing, you want to run to the phone and buy more life insurance.

Emotions are powerful messaging tools and are very useful in making an impression.

Do what the politicians do.
Talk about a real person.

"And we spent a day, a summer day, in Wise,
Virginia, with a man named James Lowe... His
amazing story, though, gave this campaign voice:
universal health care for every man, woman and
child in America. That is our cause."
—John Edwards, January 30, 2008.

Do you know a person who embodies everything good about your topic? If so, make them part of your presentation.

You might have to pay them royalties or at least tell them that you are using them as fodder for your next seminar, but I bet they'll be flattered. Who wouldn't be?

Let's say you are delivering a topic on punctuality. Got someone in your family who makes it a point to be on time? Who had to run over 5 old ladies in traffic just to get to an event at the appointed hour?

Get your topic in mind and then think about all of the people in your life from kindergarten until the present day. I guarantee that you will come up with someone that illustrates a point you want to make.

If I ever have the chance to talk to business owners about what to look for in a good controller, I'll build my presentation around a real person—Rick Burtt. Here's his story.

"Why every business needs a Rick Burtt Controller."

Rick was the Controller at Navision Software. As controller, Rick was also the gatekeeper I had to go through in order to execute any of my ideas—or at least the ones that required funding.

Rick was not in the habit of approving any idea that came down the pike. In fact, just like any good controller, he would swiftly (and loudly) turn down any idea that he disagreed with.

What makes Rick my *ideal controller* is what he did *after* he said no. He would proceed to think about the idea until he came up with a workable way for me to accomplish whatever outcome I was trying to achieve.

Rick would help me change my plan so it was better (and within budget) and then he would become a partner in my success. Most controllers could learn a lot from Rick Burtt.

Like Rick Burtt, you can decide which risks are worth taking to reach your goals.

Narrating stories with emotions and real people can feel risky, but the payoff can be wonderful for both you and your audience. Be willing to take risks with storytelling—and also be willing to put the work into shaping your story so it fits your purpose perfectly.

SIMPLIFY COMPLEX IDEAS
USING PEACHES AND BASKETBALLS

Concrete Items Can Help You Connect

Sometimes it's easier for people to grasp a complex or difficult message if you don't give it to them directly.

Maybe they've heard similar concepts before, and have been unable to implement them. Or perhaps your idea is so different from their normal way of thinking they just can't understand it.

That's why analogies, metaphors, and personification were invented.

These storytelling devices can help you take something unfamiliar and compare or contrast it with concepts, objects, or people that are familiar to your audience. It's just another way of connecting with your audience. Use elements of their universe to describe your universe.

Now your presentations can be as smooth as the surface of a frozen lake. You'll be a Casanova of the conference room.

32

Use substitute objects to help people find new ideas or approaches.

"You can't squeeze blood from a turnip."

"That was the hair on the camel's back."

You have been hired to create a presentation on a piece of equipment.

You talk to the people who have developed the equipment as you search to uncover a story to tell.

You're looking for a new and exciting angle that will help you convey the reasons your equipment is superior.

The problem is that most of these people have been working on this product since its inception and they just can't come up with new ideas. They are too immersed in the details of building the product to be able to see it from a new perspective.

Rather than resorting to water torture or other non-politically correct techniques in order to get them thinking, you might try creating scenarios using different objects to get their creative juices flowing.

Let's pretend that your equipment is more rugged, is safety tested and has more bells and whistles than its easier-to-use and less expensive competitor.

Try asking the team to help you compare the competing products with random food items—say a peach and a marshmallow.

One food is light and fluffy, sugary and fun to eat; the other is tasty, juicy, packed with nutrients and healthy. You can even bring in props and let the team help you with a hypothetical scenario.

Put the team on a mission to help you figure out how to get children to eat the healthy product rather than the sugary one. Have them design campaigns that will help the elementary school cafeteria manager get children to eat fewer marshmallows and more peaches.

You will be amazed at the solutions that flow when you remove the actual item from the discussion and replace it with everyday items that have similar qualities.

When you are making a presentation, the same item replacement concept can work. Title your topic the Marshmallow versus the Peach and then proceed to talk about your solution versus others and why the Peach wins.

This is a great framework for creating an unusual message that will be remembered long after the presentation ends. Don't be surprised if you get invited to make more presentations.

33

Give people a frame of reference.

*"A dragon is just a big lizard that flies
and breathes fire," said the father to
his inquisitive little boy.*

Give people a frame of reference.

In 1999 I had the pleasure of being involved in a trail-blazing technology initiative supported by the AICPA (American Institute of Certified Public Accountants) and a number of other influential accounting groups. It involved a new form of data sharing which would be applied to financial statement information.

The group consisted of a number of what can only be described as nerds (and I mean this in the most complimentary of ways). The "nerds" were immersed in this project, its related technology, and the accounting implications of it.

I was a representative of an accounting software vendor who was thinking about incorporating the technology into our product.

At the first meeting, I found myself in a sea of some of the brightest minds in accounting. These folks had all been slogging through countless details related to this solution for months. They were so immersed in the concept that they had a hard time explaining it to the rest of us.

I can remember sitting in these meetings with absolutely no idea what these people were talking about.

I also knew that I was going to have to go back to my company and convince them to add a technology that I couldn't understand, much less explain.

It was not until later that I was able to figure out what was going on.

A representative from RosettaNet delivered a presentation about his organization's similar initiative. He compared their solution to the Rosetta stone: it could make financial transactions understandable across different systems.

A-ha! I got it. Once I understood what they were doing, I was able to make the leap to our group's solution, which would similarly create a framework for electronically sharing financial statement information.

Now I needed a way to explain it to other people. I created a presentation called Digital Bridges and explained how this new solution and its common framework could be used to connect financial information that previously existed in separate "fiefdoms."

The more forward-thinking and leading-edge your idea, product or service, the more important it is that you find a way to connect it to something familiar.

34

If you can't compare, contrast.

"Not bird, nor plane nor even frog. Just little ole me, Underdog."
—Underdog

It wasn't a collection agency solution. Nor a pair of brass knuckles for your cousin Bruno. Nor an early payment discount. It was an automated reminder system for people who owe you money.

That's how I finally arrived at a description that got the point across about a Web-based receivables management application.

I backed into it by first describing what the solution was not.

When you are talking about new products, tools, or websites that address new problems, it can be hard to describe them. So start with products people know and tell them how your solution is different. Use contrast to make your point.

Have you ever tried to explain Twitter to someone who doesn't use it? Is it instant messaging? No. Is it e-mail? No. It's kind of like those paper messages inside a Hershey's kiss. It's 140 characters that you can use to share your comings and goings with people who choose to follow you (without the burden of calories or those messy chocolate fingers).

35

Use a bonehead example to teach a brainy process.

*Form the rabbit's hole by making a loop
in the rope. Take the leading line (the rabbit)
up through the hole. The "rabbit" sees a hunter,
runs around the tree (the standing line of the
rope). It goes back into the hole. Pull both
ends of the rope to finish the knot.
—From the boy scout handbook,
"How to tie a bowline knot"*

In the early days of Microsoft Windows technology, I was privileged to teach teams of mostly male construction workers how to automate project management using software … and a mouse.

Most of these men knew a heck of a lot more about project management than I will ever know, but they didn't know the concepts, theories or terminology necessary to use our software.

I love the irony in that statement. They needed to understand a bunch of terms that we (the software vendors) felt were best practices in order to automate processes that they already knew like the back of their hand.

So in a stroke of genius, the training department created some basic examples of projects that we could use to illustrate concepts.

Rather than using a detailed construction example, they used the process of baking a cake.

Now picture that if you will. Here is a 30-something female CPA (still wearing her traditional CPA attire—dopey grey suit) attempting to teach a group of 20 or so 50-something men in the middle of Mississippi how to use software by documenting the steps for baking a cake.

The beauty of this approach, in addition to giving my students excellent fodder for ridiculing their instructor, was that they paid attention to the process rather than questioning the details of each step.

Had we used a construction example initially, I would have been subjected to untold corrections regarding the type of hammer to use, the number of two-by-fours required for each cubic foot of dry wall, and the proper way to re-wire a 120 volt electrical outlet.

Instead, no one dared correct me on the order in which we should grease the pan, crack the egg, beat it, or turn on the oven.

All attendees successfully grasped the concepts of critical path and predecessor and successor relationships and I will never again make the mistake of using a ball-peen hammer when a regular one is called for.

Make your information relative.

And by "relative," I'm not talking
about your nerdy cousin.

Put your information in perspective. Give it context. Especially numbers.

If you have ever seen George Carlin play the Hippy Dippy Weatherman and give the sports scores, you know how disconcerting it can be to hear a number out of context.

As the weatherman, George Carlin would give the results of a game between the Atlanta Braves and the St. Louis Cardinals resulting in a score of "7". You didn't know if that was a winning or losing score, and which team had earned it.

That's what many accountants do with numbers.

If you have to share financial information of any kind, don't put a bunch of numbers up on a screen and expect anyone to get excited.

Use benchmarks, timelines, ratios—anything that can help your audience relate that number to other numbers.

The people who get you to sign up for a membership at the health club know how to apply this tip.

That's why they immediately convert that monthly membership fee into a daily rate and then say, *"Isn't your health worth more than the cost of one cup of coffee per day?"* Just try resisting that argument.

If you are having a hard time putting your number in perspective, you can always look to some Internet geek for help.

Just visit this website www.sensibleunits.com and type in your unit of measure and it will give you a meaningful translation. If you need to lose 50 pounds this year, it might be helpful to know that you're talking about 30 hardback copies of *Harry Potter and the Deathly Hallows*, 4.5 average domestic cats, 3.1 men's shot-puts, or 1.3 microwave ovens. Who wants to walk around carrying 1.3 microwave ovens everywhere they go?

If the cats and shot-puts don't float your boat, there are also a number of benchmarking services and tools available in the marketplace.

Trade associations often share benchmark data with their membership. Even Uncle Sam might be able to help you out. There is plenty of good (free) information from the US Bureau of Labor Statistics on their website here www.bls.gov.

Even if it takes you 22 minutes (the length of a single episode of Seinfeld) to give your numbers context, the resulting improvement in your presentation will be well worth the effort.

Personify to clarify.

"Middle age is the awkward period when
Father Time starts catching up
with Mother Nature."
—*Harold Coffin*

I had to find an interesting way to talk about the competitive advantages of one software solution over others.

And I just happened to be presenting at a conference with a basketball theme. So rather than listing all of the attributes of each solution or company and drawing comparisons, I used basketball player references.

I identified the characteristics of each software company and found a basketball player who shared those key traits. Then I talked about that player and his history and had the audience guess which competitor I was talking about.

One competitor had the equivalent of a height advantage so I found a tall but gangly basketball player and used him as evidence that the tallest doesn't always win.

One competitor had a good product but a notoriously disliked leader at its helm. So I used a talented player at Indiana University as my example. The antics of his coach, Bobby Knight, seriously reduced the player's ability to play to his full potential.

Another competitor was moving downstream from Fortune 500 clients to the mid-market. They were in unfamiliar territory.

So I found a player who didn't speak English and had not grown up playing basketball. When he got on the court he was at a complete loss. It took him years before he was able to understand the word "foul."

And then I used Dennis Rodman to talk about the problems of talented but undisciplined players who just don't succeed.

You can do this too. If you aren't a basketball fan, you can look to actors, actresses, or the characters they portray to find an interesting way to make your point.

Convey your concept
with a formula.

100 − [(# of "ums" per Minute) X (Number of Slides)] = Speaker Score

The more you can boil your message down, the more effective you will be at making it memorable for your audience.

Displaying your key message in a formula is a great way to do this. Just don't get so carried away with the mathematics that no one can follow your equation.

And if you are a winemaker, please don't destroy the magic of your elixir by spending all of your time talking about the chemical equation that is involved in the fermentation process. I have already seen that presentation and it wasn't pretty.

The Container Store uses this very simple formula as part of its employee training:

$$1 = 3$$

This formula conveys their belief that one great employee with proper training can do the work of three good employees.

The philosophy explains why they seek out the best employees to hire and pay more than minimum wage.

You can build a formula to convey almost any message and it will be memorable. After all, you can still recite the Pythagorean Theorem* which you learned in 7th grade can't you? Who's with me?

* In case you did forget, it's : $a^2 + b^2 = c^2$

TECHNICALLY SPEAKING

*Applied Technology Can Make
You More Human*

Talk about fighting fire with fire. One way to make a technical subject less intimidating and more interesting is with ... technology.

Sounds crazy doesn't it? But I'm not talking about using a technical tone or content in your presentation. After all, people don't want to know how something works, they want to be able to connect a solution to a need they have.

So when I say you should harness technology, I mean that you should leverage the Internet and look for tools, devices, and gadgets that can help you illustrate your point and connect more with your audience.

In the tips that follow, I share a few of my ideas about how to use technology to make your presentation less technical.

Incorporate Internet content into your presentation.

"The Internet is just a world passing around notes in a classroom."
—Jon Stewart

Internet content can add life to your presentation.

Just by virtue of forming a live connection to the virtual cloud, you have proven yourself to be a risk-taker.

If there is a blog that you follow, or a headline on a website that you want to show, you can incorporate a direct link in the body of your presentation. You can build your entire presentation using a series of links to different sites and images on the Web.

BUT—it's all about advanced planning. Be prepared with backup plans when your Internet connection is down. I'm sure even Al Gore has had that problem occasionally.

If you do plan to rely on Internet content create your own virtual safety net. You can store or "cache" selected Internet content on your machine so that it will be available offline. That way you will still be covered if you can't establish a live connection.

To "cache" content from an Internet Explorer 6.0 and prior browser, just select Favorites, then Add Favorite. Be sure to check the box that says "Make available offline." *NOTE: This option was removed in Internet Explorer 7.0. So much for the term "upgrade."*

If you can't access this feature or don't want to mess with constant reminders to update your cache, you can always use a screen capture to store the image of your screen in your Windows Clipboard.

Screen captures on most machines happen by pressing "ALT + Print Scrn" on the keyboard. Once the image is stored, go to a PowerPoint slide and use "CTRL V" to paste the image in a slide.

Then you can just move from slide to slide in your presentation without fretting about that Internet connection (or having to pay Al Gore any royalties for inventing the Internet).

If you plan to use a computer, have a plan B

(or a really capable assistant you can call).

*Me: "I have just poured Diet Coke in my
keyboard. What should I do?"
Technical Support: "Remove your hard drive.
Now go stand in front of a bus."*

Yes, I critically injured my laptop with Diet Coke, right before a presentation.

If this were to happen to you today and you were using a computer to make your presentation, you would have a number of technology options to rescue you (clearly you can't rely on your technical support staff.)

First, put your presentation on a USB flash drive and send it to someone else.

Second, if you are using or demonstrating software in your presentation, make sure there is a copy of the software loaded on a duplicate machine.

Obviously, the flash drive and the duplicate machine should be in attendance at your presentation. Pay no attention to the irritated stares from those people in the security line at the airport when you have to take out your *two* laptop computers.

Another way to access files from afar is with an Internet connection and some planning ahead. If you set it up ahead of time, the following services will give you remote access to another computer—say your office desktop PC.

* GoToMyPC—this service from Citrix lets you dial in remotely to your desktop and resume your presentation. This would be the best option—assuming you have a desktop, it is turned on, it has all of the applications that you need, and you have an Internet connection.

- Webex—you could have another employee back at the office open a Webex session showing the application that you need and then hand the controls over to you. But you will still need a computer and an Internet connection to make this happen.

- Yugma Skype—assuming that you have a friendly co-worker back at the office, you could have him or her share his desktop and show the application you need. This free service allows you to share your desktop with up to 10 users.

- IBM Lotus Sametime Unyte—this is a web sharing tool like all the others, but it comes from Big Blue so it has to be good. They seem to be finding new ways to apply that Lotus Notes product they acquired a while ago. They are probably hungry for market share so you might want to check it out.

Unfortunately, at the time this incident happened to me, there were no such tools and even if the tools existed, I wouldn't have been able to get an Internet connection. Be glad *you* were born after the invention of computers.

Hand out glasses—or make sure the people in the back can see your screen

They have to see it to believe it.

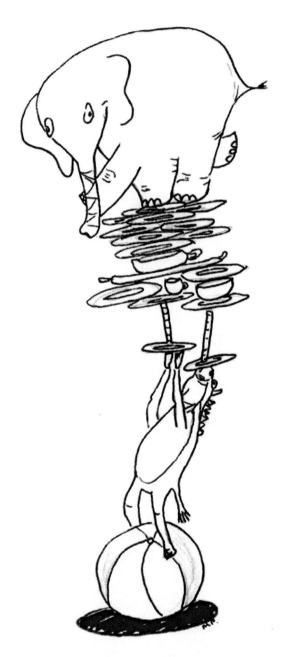

They have to see it to believe it.

Unless you are presenting in Texas, where presumably even people's contact lenses are bigger, you can use these tools to help magnify the information on screen:

* **Virtual Magnifying Glass** www.magnifier.sourceforge.net

* **Zoomit from Microsoft** www.systinternals.com

* **Click Tricks** www.southpac.com/clicktricks.htm

These are essential tools—whether you're presenting information with numbers (financial statements for example), demonstrating software, or showing anything else that's tiny and requires good eyesight.

42

Let a robot be your muse.

"Danger, Will Robinson"
—The robot on TV's Lost In Space

OK, not a robot robot like C-3PO, but a Web robot, or "bot." Bots are those magical gophers of the Internet that go out and crawl the Web in search of references and sites on a given topic.

If you are sitting deadlocked with a blank slide deck in front of you, you might give www.StumbleUpon.com a try.

StumbleUpon semi-randomly takes you to different websites. You pick the categories you're interested in, and StumbleUpon takes you to sites in those categories that have been highly rated by other Internet visitors.

Using your continuous feedback, it then refines your selections. You rate every site it suggests and eventually accumulate quite a library of interesting sites.

While many of the sites can be quite entertaining (aka a black hole), often you'll stumble, trip, or impale yourself upon something quite useful and apropos.

Perhaps you'll find a site with some shareware you can use to illustrate a point or an image that can bring home your message. You can quickly stroll through a number of different sites, any number of which could provide you with instant inspiration.

Disclaimer: Do not blame me if you become addicted to the StumbleUpon process and are forced to increase your dosage of Ritalin as a result of its adverse impact on your A.D.D.

A definition of Bot, from Wikipedia

"Internet bots, also known as web robots, WWW robots or simply bots, are software applications that run automated tasks over the Internet.

Typically, bots perform tasks that are both simple and structurally repetitive, at a much higher rate than would be possible for a human alone.

The largest use of bots is in web spidering, in which an automated script fetches, analyzes and files information from web servers at many times the speed of a human."

Insert freebies.

*Read "Free Prize Inside: The Next Big
Marketing Idea," by Seth Godin.*

I often make presentations on behalf of one company or another and I usually have a list of products that I demonstrate during the course of my session.

But, I always try to show other free products or shareware that everyone in the audience can use— without having to buy any of the products I cover. It's always nice when people leave your session talking about some free piece of software they can play with at home.

Some of my favorite freebies:

* Bullfighter software from www.fightthebull.com helps you locate and remove the "bull" from your writing. This also makes for a great demonstration when you pick a piece of well-designed writing and show the bull score that it earns.

* www.Weebly.com for building free websites.

* Virtual Magnifying Glass from magnifier.sourceforge.net is shareware that gets mentioned twice in my book because it is so cool (and because I have no life). This tool helps you enlarge the images you are showing on screen. People always get excited about this one.

* GIMP from www.gimp.org is really good graphics software available as shareware (that means free).

* Google desktop from of course, www.google.com, is a free desktop search engine. Stop trying to remember the name of that folder that stores your critical documents, just type in a keyword and let Google search your desktop—lightning fast.

ENGAGING YOUR AUDIENCE

Make the Relationship Last

You don't have to worry about getting down on one knee, but you should be worried about getting your audience involved in your presentation.

If you want to deliver a monologue, you might want to consider drama instead of presenting. The real power of a great presenter comes when he is able to draw energy from his interactions with the audience.

Let people get hands-on with the information.

*There's a reason the sandbox is a
favorite choice at playtime.*

Which would you prefer? Would you rather sit through a half-hour explanation of how fun it is to play with Play-dough™ or have someone hand you a chunk of pink dough and let you mess with it for a while?

Your presentation attendees are no different from you. When you let people sink their teeth into concepts—rather than just listen to you talking about them—they are more likely to really understand.

Imagine your mission is to teach banking concepts to a room full of small business owners who are looking to get loans. Or you have a room full of high school students in a junior achievement class who want to learn about finances.

Either way, it will be more fun for everyone involved if they have a chance to interact with the information rather than just listen.

Go over some basic concepts, explain credit criteria, and throw in the Altman Z score* for good measure.

Then pass out sample financial statements and Monopoly money and let your attendees decide who gets a loan based on the criteria you have covered.

You will be amazed at the number of people who pull out pencils and paper and try to make the best decision.

Talk about a memorable presentation. Pass out pocket calculators and slide rules to really crank up the fun.

* Doesn't everyone know what the Altman Z score is?

Okay, here it is : The Altman Z score is a tool used to predict the likelihood of bankruptcy. A score lower than 2 indicates a potential business continuity concern.

$$Z = 1.2A + 1.4B + 3.3C + 0.6D + 1.0E$$

Where:

Z = Score

A = Working Capital/Total <u>Assets</u>

B = Retained Earnings/Total Assets

C = Earnings Before Interest & Tax/Total Assets

D = <u>Market Value</u> of Equity/Total Liabilities

E = Sales/Total Assets

Ask questions.

"Why?"
— Any two-year old

Meet your audience before you start speaking. Find out why they are attending your session and what they are looking to learn. See if they have any particular issues they want you to cover.

And sprinkle your presentation with questions. Stop and ask the audience for input. If you had a chance to meet someone during the warm up, call them by name and refer to something they told you about their business. Incorporate that into your topic.

Attend other presenter's sessions to get a feel for what others are saying. Even better if you can use a reference or specific phrase from a preceding presentation and relate it to your topic.

In comedy, this technique is called a "callback." This tip requires you to actually stay awake in other sessions and pay enough attention to snag a pertinent tie-in to your material.

If the speakers before you are especially boring, that gives you an even better shot at really making an impact with your presentation. Of course, if you would like to help them jazz up their message, you know where to send them.

46

Use more audience interactions with a small crowd.

"Just you 'n me, simple and free"
—Chicago

When you have a small, intimate group, you have an opportunity to change the nature of your presentation so it is more personal.

Even if you have spent the last 2 months preparing hundreds of the most gorgeous slides in the world, you might want to switch to a less formal discussion.

There is nothing more pitiful than watching a presenter slog through his 100 PowerPoint slides to a room with two people situated as far back in the room as possible.

You are far better off trying to target your presentation to the exact needs of those two people and foster a dialogue between them and you.

You might discover that they are there to hear exactly what you planned to cover, or you might learn that they are really only interested in one small item that is covered on slide 42 of your deck.

Whatever the case, take the time to find out who you have in the room and adjust your presentation accordingly.

Be a facilitator.

"When I give up trying to impress the group, I become very impressive. Let go in order to achieve. The wise facilitator speaks rarely and briefly, teaching more through being than doing."
—From The Tao

Let the audience make your points for you.

Provide input sheets to capture their thoughts, and display them on a sticky note pad on the wall. Then organize the information and talk about whatever point you are trying to make.

I suppose you want me to give you an example.

Okay, say your subject is "Revenue versus Cash" and you are teaching business executives about some accounting concepts.

Start your presentation by asking them to write down one example of a cash-based transaction in their business and place it on a sticky note.

Then ask everyone in the room to place their sticky notes on the wall.

Now you go up and arrange the sticky notes in different groups for sales, deposits, loans, insurance proceeds, etc.

You'll quickly be able to make your point—not all cash that flows into a business is revenue.

People love to see their ideas used. With a bit of quick thinking you can harness your audience's input to get your message across.

SHARE THE STAGE

*Unless the World Really Does
Revolve Around You*

One of the best things to learn as a presenter is when to be silent.

You need to make a realistic assessment before you agree to make a presentation. Maybe there are other people who are better able to deliver the message for you. Or perhaps your client wants to have a chance to speak in front of your audience.

It could be that you don't resonate with a particular audience, or maybe you need to cover a technical concept that is outside of your area of expertise.

That would be the time to make yourself look like the professional you are by applying the tips that follow.

Swing your partner.

"Mom always liked you best"
—Tommy Smothers,
"The Smothers Brothers Comedy Hour"

Just like a well rehearsed square dance, some of the best presentations I have seen involved two speakers.

Often the individuals weren't great presenters by themselves but by combining two average speakers in the right forum you ended up with a great presentation. They would each play to their strengths and use the contrast in topic and manner to get their point across.

Other times, two presenters would share the stage, with one of them being dynamic and the other less so. Everyone would be rooting for the less dynamic of the two to score a few digs at his co-presenter. The resulting tension made for a spell-binding presentation.

So don't be afraid to team up with a partner. Rehearsing your material in advance to ensure smooth flow will be extremely important, but the added value of conversational banter that results from having multiple presenters will be worth the effort.

49

Don't say a word.

"Like my body?"
—Anna Nicole Smith in Trimspa commercial

Let other people tell your story.

Rather than standing in front of an audience and telling them about your great product, idea, or service, bring up actual customers who have benefited from your solution.

They can tell your story in a far more believable way and your audience will be far more likely to trust them.

If your audience is salespeople and you want to educate them on the benefits of a new CRM* system, for example, find other salespeople you can put on a panel to share their insights.

If you must be in the spotlight, then become the moderator of the event and generate some insightful questions for your panelists. Just be sure to give them ample time to make all of your points for you.

* Customer Relationship Management

SPECIAL DELIVERY, ANYONE?

Return Receipt Requested

A sk any hungry pizza patron what's important and they'll tell you delivery. The same is true for presentations.

The bulk of this guide has been devoted to ideas that help you generate interesting content. And of course that is important.

But, the most exciting topic in the world can be turned into a boring one with bad delivery. At the same time a boring subject can be drastically improved with an animated delivery.

So once you have that killer idea ready to roll (or should I say ready to slide), take the time to consider the tips that follow.

50

Practice—know that content inside and out.

"Just do it."
— Nike

If you have a boring topic to begin with, you need to have a stellar delivery to help amp up the excitement. And practice is the only way to get better.

Volunteer at every opportunity until you are comfortable in front of an audience. Have your friends listen to you giving your presentation—reviewing your content silently in your head doesn't count.

Say it out loud and time yourself. Record your voice as you present—can you detect passion and energy in your voice? If not, you need to find a different way to share your message until you find one that lights your fire.

One of the best things I learned from Stand Up Comedy training was rehearsing by recording my routine into a tape recorder.

I was commuting 2.5 hours from work to home at the time so I had plenty of time to listen to my poorly delivered routines. But by the time I got to my destination, I knew my material and had perfected the nuances of timing that are so critical to comedy.

(But gosh, was I sick of hearing that southern accent. I swear I don't talk like that in real life!)

So go find yourself a padded room and practice your delivery.

Take control of your space.

"Space the final frontier"
—Star Trek
(did I mention I am a nerd?)

Do not in any circumstance treat the podium as your shield protecting you from the audience. (But it *would* be really cool if you could get one of those force fields like they use in Star Trek.)

If you have a boring subject and you plant yourself at the podium, cowering and immobile, you are only going to doom your presentation to the annals of the boring.

One of the tools you have available to you as the presenter is space. Use the space in the room to your advantage.

Make sure that your microphone supports movement as you don't want to be remembered as the presenter who tripped over the cord, or the person who was flopped back to the front of the room when he reached the limits of his microphone bungee cord.

If you want to get your audience engaged, then move out among them. They can't ignore you or continue typing text messages to their friends when you are standing right in front of them.

They will be stunned and alert by virtue of your proximity to their chair. And they will have no choice but to answer any questions that you pose.

Be sure to visit the back of the room so you can wake those people up. They thought they were going to get off easy and sneak out early by hiding in the back.

But if you get them involved in your presentation, they are going to want to stay until the end and see what else you have in store for your session.

And if you are presenting in a long room, an extra bonus is the workout you get from going back and forth between the audience and your computer.

Or you can invest in a remote mouse if you can find one that works reliably. I haven't had good luck with these. I am often showing live software demonstrations so I end up having to go back to my laptop to resume my presentation.

Which reminds me—the setup of the room is very important if you plan to roam about. You don't want to be roaming directly into the light of the projector so be sure to take your planned hike into account when you are setting up the room.

52

Take speaker training classes.

*"If you think education is expensive,
try ignorance."*
—Derek Bok

People who have energy and passion when they speak can read from a phone book and make it sound interesting.

The professionals at Speechworks, www.Speechworks.net, based in Atlanta, Georgia can teach you how to deliver your information with passion. They offer an amazing number of courses and have a great presentation methodology that you can put to use in any form of communication.

They can also help you make an impact with your voice and body. Their training classes include video-taping and coaching from former television personalities who really know how to engage an audience.

I have attended a couple of their training courses and I cannot say enough about the benefits.

There is so much value to seeing yourself on camera. As I recall, the feedback I received in one class included something about looking like a preacher talking about fire and brimstone. (Who knew that growing up across the street from a Baptist College would rub off on me.)

In watching the tape, it was true that I got pretty passionate about one of the subjects I delivered—I'm pretty sure it must have had something to do with food.

The training not only helped me in making presentations, but it also helped my confidence in daily interactions. If I had not taken their training, I also would have never known that one side of my mouth appears to be suffering from a stroke when I speak.

I don't know if I am trying to save energy by only using half of my mouth, but it is darn scary to see on film. And I'm not sure how to correct it since it is involuntary, but I am glad to know which side of the audience I should face at my next presentation.

CLOSING

No matter how boring or dry your subject, I know you will find a way to make it interesting.

You have the tools and you know your subject matter. You've taken the time to think, plan, and get to know your audience.

Besides, how can you fail now that you have 52 tips? That's one for each week of the year.

But if you do happen to get stuck and you are running out of time for that big presentation, go to www.evenanerd.com and send me an e-mail. I will talk you down from the ledge. Maybe we'll both learn something.

Although this book stops here, great ideas for presentations have no end. (I'm sorry to say.) Get a monthly injection of new presentation ideas at my free monthly webinars. Go to www.evenanerd.com to sign up. And while you're there, drop me an e-mail. I'd love to know about your presentations and how you applied these tips.

Now go forth and eliminate boring from the world.

Appendix

Other books on presentations and communication:

* *Even a Geek Can Speak* by Joey Asher

* *Juicy Pens, Thirsty Paper* by SARK

* *Slide:ology: The Art and Science of Creating Great Presentations* by Nancy Duarte

* *Clear and to the Point: 8 Psychological Principles for Compelling PowerPoint Presentations* by Stephen M. Kosslyn

* *Understanding Comics: The Invisible Art* by Scott McCloud

* *Thinking Visually* by Mark Wigan

* *Presentation Zen* by Garr Reynolds

* *Really Bad PowerPoint (and how to avoid it)* by Seth Godin

* *Bird by Bird: Some Instructions on Writing and Life* by Anne Lamott

* *The Naked Brain* by Richard Restak, M.D.

Acknowledgements

I know it is only a small book but it felt bigger. It wouldn't have existed at all without the support of a lot of people over the years.

Thank you Beth, Stacy, Kellie and all of my nerdy friends (you know who you are) who listened to me, laughed with me, and believed I could really do this.

Thank you to Lynn, Jess, and Frank Greer who taught me how to play with others and have always been there to hold the net just below me. Well, except for that time I fell out of the tree.

Much credit and thanks goes to my editor Amy Moore. "Moore Words" or less words, they were always the right words.

Thank you to Mike Woods at Deloitte who taught me the biggest lesson I needed to learn about communication.

Thank you to Betsy Burroughs who blazed the trail that led to this book and held my hand while I walked down it.

Thank you to Mom who showed me that there are no limits and that yes, you can glue fabric to the ceiling if you keep trying. And to Dad, who taught me to love numbers, tax books, and ice cream sandwiches and inspired me to be funny at his funeral.

Thank you to Randy Keith and Rick Burtt who let me be part of the company that ignited my passion for speaking.

Thank you to Carlton Collins who showed me how a professional delivers a great presentation.

Thank you to Sage Software, the first investor in my small business.

Thank you to all of my clients who don't take themselves too seriously and who allow me to play on their behalf.

Thank you, Jeff Justice, for showing me how to deliver those five minutes at the Punchline without embarrassing myself on stage.

Thank you, Edi and Steve Osborne, for letting me be part of your amazing tribe.

Thank you to Jim Metzler, one of the original accountants with a personality and the first CPA-author I met.

Thank you Mary Patterson, the illustrating bookkeeper, for your art work.

Thank you to Brian Austin at Speedtax who has treated me like a famous author all of these years.

Thank you Charles, my caregiver, sidekick, partner, supporter, source of material for stand-up comedy, and constant believer, I love you.

And none of this would have happened had it not been for a book written by Joey Asher at SpeechWorks, called *Even a Geek Can Speak*. Joey answered his phone that day I called him, the second I finished reading it, and he hasn't been able to get rid of me since.

CPSIA information can be obtained at www.ICGtesting.com
Printed in the USA
BVOW04s1854020215

386046BV00017B/409/P